John Farman's birth in 1944 heralded the downfall of Adolf Hitler. Son of the famous Spanish painter Pablo Farman, he showed the same autistic leanings from an early age. He went on to study at the Royal College of Art where he had the distinction of being the only student with a spaniel.

First published 1989 by Pan Books Ltd
Cavaye Place, London SW10 9PG

9 8 7 6 5 4 3 2 1

© John Farman 1989

Illustrations © John Farman 1989

ISBN 0 330 31272 3

Printed and bound in Great Britain by
BPCC Hazell Books Ltd
Member of BPCC Ltd
Aylesbury, Bucks, England

You can't tell a rook by its cover.

This book is intended for all those people whose life is a continual search for truth. The following proverbs have been painstakingly researched by the author, an internationally respected English Skolar.

Unreliable proverbs from John Farman.

WILHELM CHWEITZER, the philosopher and recluse, spent much of his childhood trying to find quiet places to think. It is now known that he resorted to spending hours on end in the lavatory, much to the concern of his parents (to whom he had never spoken).

Believing that he suffered severe constipation, they gave poor Willy laxatives at every opportunity, so that what had been a ruse to get away from his noisy family, now became a necessity. So much so that in later life his thinking became synonymous with visiting the toilet and vice versa.

When he died it came to light that all his major works, including *Universal thinking from a confined space*, were written in his specially converted loo.

It is a fitting tribute to this great man that his initials are now common parlance.

Great minds like a think

DURING the Great Newt Uprising of 1953, a group of the grossly enlarged amphibians tore through the sleepy market town of Saffron Walden, raping, pillaging and generally making a nuisance of themselves. Owing to their remarkable fleetness of foot, coupled with the doziness of the local constabulary, they were never caught and consequently never brought to book.

Bad newts travel fast

CYRIL RAMSBOTTOM of Ashton under Lyne is generally regarded as the inventor of the modern hairpiece or toupée.

The discovery occurred when all his hitherto lustrous hair fell out following a horrible accident in his own front drive. Cyril carelessly reversed his new car, a Standard Vanguard, over the sleeping body of his tom-cat Leon.

So as never to forget his dear, departed and flattened pet (and to keep his newly denuded head warm), he tied Leon's feet under his chin and was never seen in public, henceforward, without him.

If the cat fits wear it

BRAITHWAITE'S DOVE was discovered by Charles St John Braithwaite in 1837 when he was exploring the rain forests of New Guinea.

Whilst moving through particularly dense undergrowth he heard a muted squawk. Under the heel of his boot he found a small bird the like of which he had never seen before. He wondered why it hadn't made its escape when it saw him coming. On closer examination he found it had no eyes and only rudimentary ears.

After exhaustive searches lasting twenty-seven years he failed to find another like it and died of a horrid tropical disease, taking to his grave the knowledge that he'd probably trodden on the last one.

Dove is Blind

THE nature of nuns' undergarments has always been a closely guarded secret within the walls of the convent, leading to all kinds of imaginative speculation about naughty nun's knickers and mother superior's suspenders.

The makers of the recent blockbuster film, *A Habit for Loving*, discovered the truth by slipping an actress in to the convent at Oswaldtwistle, Lancs. as an undercover novice. Now catapulted to fame for her moving portrayal of Sister Kate's 'unfrocking', Samantha Starr said of her convent experience, 'I'd like to thank the sisters of Oswaldtwistle for baring their lives and souls to me as they did.' The Mother Superior refused comment on the authenticity of the depiction of nuns' lives in the film.

There's nothing new under the nun

THE little church of St Peregrine in deepest Bedfordshire hasn't had a heating bill for years. Why the place stays so warm has been a mystery to all the faithful.

Rumour has it, however, that in 1743 there was a certain parson by the name of Oswald de Vere Ponsonby-Cleat, who was suspected of being a devil worshipper. The legend goes that one night he even invited the rascal into his church.

This would account for the perfect scorched impression of a goat's bum on the old corner pew, and the strange warmth that always seems to radiate from it.

Give the devil his pew

FREDERICK and Charlene Delgardo of Phoenix, Arizona caused a small sensation when they opened an establishment wherein very old men could, for a small consideration, embrace the nubile staff under strict medical supervision. Apart from the odd coronary it was so successful that local doctors noticed a remarkable decline in illnesses among male patients over seventy-five. The premises, called Freddie's Feel-Eazy, were unfortunately burnt down by an irate female pensioner whose demands for similar facilities for women were defeated by opposition from local Boy Scout groups.

A man is as old as <u>she</u> feels

WHEN children sing 'While shepherds wash their socks by night', they may not necessarily be blaspheming. Exhaustive research has shown that this might well be the original version.

Around the time of Christ's birth shepherds were notoriously filthy. So foul, in fact, that their charges often got lost on purpose to escape the rancid odours.

It was only when those now-famous shepherds heard that they'd been selected to visit the new Messiah, that they pulled their fingers out and changed their clothes. Their socks apparently were so high that they nearly walked to Nazareth by themselves.

A shepherd does not change his socks

ROLAND SMAIL was obsessed by his hobby of building models in bottles. Bored with trains and boats and planes, he decided to investigate the possibility of growing a living creature in a big old port bottle. For months he studied all the latest research papers on transplant technology. Using a pig's embryo donated by a farmer friend, he managed, incredibly, to raise a piglet by feeding it intravenously through the bottle's neck. Unfortunately he was never able to reconcile the young porker's need for food with the inevitable growth that followed.

Curiously, Mr Smail was found dead beside a healthy, if somewhat hungry piglet. The autopsy showed him to have died under a hail of glass splinters.

You cannot put new swine
in old bottles.

WHEN the fad for keeping baby alligators in the aquaria of smart New York apartments ended in the late 1970s, many were released into the sewers where they flourished in the warm, dark atmosphere. There are now reported to be more of these huge reptiles under the streets of Manhattan than in the rest of the world.

Recently the New York police have been baffled by the growing number of people disappearing while in the smallest room. There is even a public service warning on all major TV networks advising citizens to check inside their 'johns' before use.

Look before you leak

BRIAN, the only blind horse in Toytown, was extremely depressed and needed to talk to someone who had survived a difficult period in their lives. He heard that Noddy, a local gnome, had been the subject of press reports alleging a homosexual relationship with Big Ears, his long-time friend.

Noddy, untroubled by these malicious rumours, turned out to be extremely wise and helped Brian realise that things could be much worse. They got on so well in fact that they set up home together (much to Big Ears' distress) and are said to be very happy.

Noddy's as good as a shrink to a blind horse

THERE was once a famous Soho restaurant called Uncle Jacob's Fishcoteque. It was so popular that Jacob decided to open another restaurant nearby. This one was more upmarket, serving an international cuisine.

Jacob's regular customers were furious when they discovered that not only was the new place not kosher, but pork was the speciality dish! Word went round and soon the whole of the Jewish community boycotted and picketed both establishments.

Both restaurants were forced to close down; but, never being one to miss a gap in the market, Jacob opened a factory producing Uncle Jacob's Kosher Sausages (made from cod).

You cannot serve cod
and gammon

ONE of our smallest and best-loved British birds is the wren. Though unremarkable in most respects the wren has one particular idiosyncrasy that distinguishes it from all other birds of the *Troglodyte* family. It suffers when young from acute flatulence, which is probably due to being fed almost exclusively on the larvae of the greater bean weevil (*Beannus Baccus*).

The great Russian Ornithologist Vladimir Titsky stumbled across this interesting fact through noticing that whenever he was in the vicinity of a nest of wrens he heard strange little high-pitched wiffling noises accompanied by a rather unpleasant sulphurous odour. The discovery formed the basis for Titsky's famous and oft-quoted paper, which became the definitive work on the subject.

The nest of wrens must fart

IVY GRIPPET'S ten-year-old cat Rambo suffered a particularly unpleasant demise when he leapt into the grill to devour the bloater intended for Mr Grippet's supper. All was not lost, thank goodness, as Mrs Grippet kindly gave her husband hers and had a boiled egg instead.

Curiosity grilled the cat

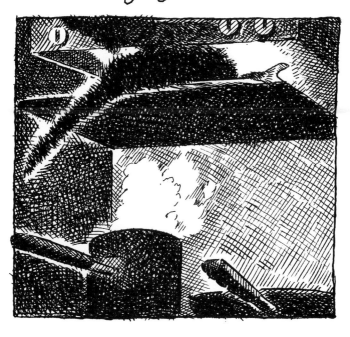

IT is a little known fact that weevils (family *Carculionidae*) have very little natural insulation from the cold. This explains why they spend most of their wretched little lives burrowing into things. The net result of all this is that the poor weevil has almost continual coughs and colds and a permanently runny nose.

Runny is the snoot of all weevils

MELANIE SMELT of Darlington recently sued her hairdresser Maurice (Clive Gorringe), of Julian and Maurice Hair Modes, in the local magistrate's court. She claimed she'd asked for something 'bold'. The defendant replied that Miss Smelt had a slight speech impediment and that as his previous client had been a skinhead, he'd misunderstood her request.

The magistrate found against the plaintiff, saying that anyone can make a mistake. He asked, completely off the record, whether Maurice ever accepted male clients.

Hell hath no fury like
a woman shorn

IT is generally believed that mules, being hybrid, cannot breed. The truth is they can, but they make dreadfully bad parents, forgetting to feed their offspring from the minute they're born.

Next time your mule has a nipper make sure to remove it immediately in order to find a surrogate parent.

This is much easier than one might imagine, as mules, being not that bright, can't seem to tell the difference. As the ancient rhyme tells us:

> When you have to take a hand
> In nature's wondrous scheme,
> And seize the offspring of your mule
> To start a new regime –
> Although the search for the right mum
> Might seem a little gruelling;
> It must be said that as a rule
> You'll fool the mewling mule-ling.

A mule and its mummy are soon parted

BOTH Harry and Gladys McDick had had very sheltered upbringings. In fact, neither had ever been told the facts of life. Thus they were highly mystified when, after many years of marriage, they realised that their once-spacious Glasgow bedsitter was becoming rather crowded.

With a view to getting to the bottom of this dilemma they sought the advice of the local social services.

As always the experts went straight to the root of the problem . . . and rehoused them in a larger flat.

Small things come to those who mate

STAVROS AGAMEMNON, the famous Greek animal trainer, bored with lions, tigers and bears, was looking for something different.

His technique of punishment, followed by reward, had always been successful, so when he applied it to his seven new pythons he genuinely expected good results.

Having trained them to go rigid so that he could juggle and balance spinning plates on them, he managed to get them to spell his name right across the ring. It was when he started planning the first reptilian high wire act that the snakes rebelled and no further punishment could persuade them.

Poor Stavros was found one morning squeezed lifeless by his charges. His coffin was said to be only one foot wide, but eleven feet long.

You can't have your snake
and beat it

SID SNATCH, leader of the Vomit Brothers, the most notorious of the punk bands of the 1970s, had an appalling secret. His pale, sickly and incredibly spotty countenance was cosmetic, arrived at after hours of painstaking work.

When he got home in the evening he would throw off his studded leather clothes and slip into a sports jacket, a pair of slacks, a Viyella shirt and a Paisley cravat (with toggle). He would then make a cup of Ovaltine and relax to his favourite Roger Whittaker album.

When he went missing, his fans cheerfully assumed he'd abused himself to death. Rumour has it however that Snatch is alive and very well thank you, having traded in guitar-bashing and vomit for that blandest of jobs – writing incredibly successful West End musicals – and bringing his previously hidden lifestyle, literally, out of the closet.

Better to be envied than pitted

YOUR common or garden bunny rabbit (*Lepus Cuniculus*) breeds no fewer than seven times a year. This puts an enormous physical and mental strain on the burrowhold.

It has now been established that among the highly sophisticated rabbit communities there is usually one senior member who acts as a kind of therapist to the others. It is mostly the males who need help, as it appears that their female counterparts become very cold and unfeeling towards their mates (who can blame them?) – and often go to the bunny burial place hard and embittered and hating just about everyone (even Richard Adams).

Old rabbits die hard

ABSINTHE is a liqueur distilled from wine and wormwood (a substance used in the treatment of intestinal worms). Although aniseedy and pleasant to the taste, it is incredibly potent and capable of causing brain damage. It is also reputed to have aphrodisiac qualities.

In 1949 Jean-Pierre Lecoq was found deftly dismembered behind a back-street bar in the Pigalle district of Paris. At the inquest it transpired that he was murdered by persons unknown, seemingly in revenge for his dishonest habit of getting the local streetwalkers so drunk on the dreaded absinthe, that they let him have his way for nothing.

Absinthe makes the tart grow fonder

SHARON THRELFALL of Slough was a full-time shorthand secretary, and a part-time fetishist. Her office manager, Leonard Beamish, though not averse to a little after work 'correction', drew the line at some of the more extreme outfits she wore to work.

As a compromise she was allowed to wear her extremely uncomfortable underwear beneath her office clothes. These consisted of chains and leather thongs held together by small padlocks. Leonard kept the keys to the padlocks in his pending file – along with a small telescopic whip and his lunchbox.

A chain is as good as a vest

HUGH FLANGE, deacon of St Jude's, Ashbourne loved his Morris Minor estate, Jezebel, more than his wife and kids and some say more than God. Unfortunately his meagre stipend didn't run to having a garage built next to his little cottage and he hated leaving his 'treasure' to the mercy of the elements.

A few of his faithful parishioners, hearing his fervent prayers through the vestry door, decided to organize a collection. They had the garage built while he was away on ecclesiastical business.

Although astonished and thrilled, on his return, at the quick response to his prayers, Flange was rather miffed that the garage didn't have the electrically-operated doors he'd requested.

Garages are made in heaven

IT is a little known but remarkable fact that the common stoat (*Putorius Erminius*) is the only mammal capable of not only producing rennet (a well known coagulant), but also of transferring this substance into its own bloodstream at will. Consequently, owing to extreme viscidity of its blood, our stoat has very little fear of injury from sharp objects or the teeth of predators.

Even when cut up into very small pieces the stoat refuses to relinquish one drop of blood. In fact its rather cavalier attitude to violence makes it far more feared than its size would warrant.

You can't get blood out
of a stoat

A YOUNG hippie, Tristram Jelineck, from St Ives in Cornwall, discovered that dried dandelion leaves (commonly known as *pissenlit* in France), when smoked, tasted very much like marijuana. Realizing the enormous financial potential he decided to collect every last dandelion in the area. When he had filled the back of his Transit van (which he lived in), he hot-footed to London and sold his innocuous product to all his friends who thought it the best 'gear' they'd ever got hold of.

The idea might have caught on had it not been for its embarrassing side effect which the French have known about for centuries.

A friend in weed is a
friend indeed

HERBERT MATTHEWS, an East Anglian farmer, had a theory that if he could combine the taste and texture of chicken with the breeding capabilities of fish he would not only solve the world's nutrition problem but would also become extremely rich into the bargain. Business never really got off the ground, unfortunately, owing to nearly all his cockerels drowning at the breeding stage. Those which survived appeared decidedly unenamoured of the fish.

One man's meat is another man's poisson

BRENDA CROWTHORPE from Huddersfield had been dating Neville Trundle for nearly ten years. The one thorn in their otherwise rosy relationship was Brenda's embarrassment over Neville's rather strange dress sense. Reluctant to comment for fear of offending Neville, Brenda kept her thoughts to herself. But every year when he asked her to marry him she refused saying there was something about him she was not quite sure of.

While browsing through the personal column of the *Huddersfield Bugle* she happened upon an ad which read:

Novice transvestite seeks understanding girl to advise on fashion, make-up and men. Serious replies only please.

Feeling compassion for the young man's plight and seeing an outlet for her repressed passion for fashion, Brenda replied to the ad only to find out that it was her Neville who'd placed it. They're now happily married and sharing Brenda's elegant and tasteful wardrobe.

Better the Neville you know
than the Neville you don't

ERNEST GROUT had been a sleepwalker since childhood. Apart from the inconvenience of never quite knowing where he was going to wake up, he lived with the problem reasonably happily.

In the court case between Mrs Enid Grout and the local housing authority, the former won considerable damages as a result of her husband's untimely and traumatic death. Their enforced rehousing from bungalow to towerblock had had severe and far-reaching consequences.

Don't change houses in mid dream

THE summer of 1958 saw, in Knoxville, Tennessee, a remarkable contest to find the stupidest man in the state. The finalists were one Walter Gristle, a turkey inseminator, and Bud Winklebaum, a guinea-pig at the local germ-warfare research laboratory.

Walt lost the contest when, to everyone's surprise, he remembered his name. Bud was delighted with his prize of a week's all-inclusive holiday in a volcano.

Sadly, he never got to go owing to his untimely death from sniffing an exciting new gas which the company, thrilled with its virulence, named after him as a mark of respect.

Bud is thicker than Walter